COMPREHENSION SKILLS

MAIN IDEA

LEVEL C

Linda Ward Beech

Tara McCarthy

Donna Townsend

STECK-VAUGHN
ELEMENTARY · SECONDARY · ADULT · LIBRARY

A Harcourt Company

www.steck-vaughn.com

Editorial Director:	Diane Schnell
Project Editor:	Anne Souby
Associate Director of Design:	Cynthia Ellis
Design Manager:	Cynthia Hannon
Media Researcher:	Christina Berry
Production:	Karen Wilburn
Cover Illustration:	Stephanie Carter
Cover Production:	Alan Klemp
Photograph:	©PhotoDisc

ISBN 0-7398-2637-9

12 13 14 15   170   10 09

The main idea is the point a writer wants to make in a story. In this book you will learn about main ideas.

Look at the picture on this page. It was taken at an airport. You can see the airplanes. You can see the baggage cars. The airport is the main idea. The airplanes and baggage cars are details that add interest to the airport.

What Is a Main Idea?

The main idea of a story tells what it is about. The other sentences add details to the main idea. Often the main idea is stated in the first or last sentence of the paragraph. Sometimes you may find the main idea in the middle of the paragraph.

This example may help you think about main ideas:

$$5 + 6 + 7 = 18$$

detail + detail + detail = main idea

The *5*, *6*, and *7* are like details. They are smaller than their sum, *18*. The *18*, like a main idea, is bigger. It is made of several smaller parts.

Try It!

Read the story below. Draw a line under the main idea.

Jazz is an American form of music. Jazz was first based on the work songs of slaves. It began in the South and spread to other parts of the country.

The main idea sentence is the first sentence in the story. All the other sentences are details. They give more facts about jazz.

The main idea could come at the end of the story:

Jazz was first based on the work songs of slaves. It began in the South and spread to other parts of the country. Jazz is an American form of music.

Using What You Know

The main idea is often someone's opinion, not a fact. A writer uses details to convince a reader that his or her opinion is the correct one.

Read the main ideas on this page. Each main idea is an opinion. Write some detail sentences that support the main idea. The first one is done for you.

Main Idea: Summer is the best time of year.

Detail: You don't have to go to school.

Detail: You have time to play with your friends.

Detail: You can go swimming every day.

Main Idea: Fiction is more interesting than nonfiction.

Detail: _____

Detail: _____

Detail: _____

Main Idea: To be happy you need to have friends.

Detail: _____

Detail: _____

Detail: _____

Main Idea: It is exciting to go on vacations.

Detail: _____

Detail: _____

Detail: _____

Main Idea: Playing outside is more fun than playing inside.

Detail: _____

Detail: _____

Detail: _____

Practice Finding the Main Idea

This book asks you to find main ideas. Read the story and the question below.

◆

There are more than three thousand kinds of frogs. The grass frog is so small it can sit on an acorn. The goliath frog of West Africa is the largest frog in the world. It is the size of a cat. The water-holding frog uses the skin it has shed to make a bag around itself. This bag holds in water and keeps the frog cool.

C **1.** The story mainly tells
    A. about the goliath frog
    B. about a tiny frog
    C. that there are many kinds of frogs
    D. about the water-holding frog

The correct answer is **C**. The story includes details about three kinds of frogs. These details support the first sentence.

Sometimes a story does not have a main idea sentence. You can figure out the main idea by reading the details. Read the story below.

◆

The Sahara Desert is found in North Africa. The desert gets from five to ten inches of rain a year. But sometimes there are dry periods that last years. The temperature may reach 135 degrees during the day.

2. The story mainly tells
    A. how hot the Sahara is
    B. facts about the Sahara
    C. where the Sahara is found
    D. how much rainfall the Sahara gets

To check your answer, turn to page 60.

How to Use This Book

This book has 25 units. Each unit has 5 stories. In units
1 through 12, the stories have main idea sentences. In units 13
through 25, the stories do not have main idea sentences. Read
the stories and answer the questions. Write the letters of the
correct answers in the blanks.

When you finish, check your answers on pages 61 and 62.
Tear out the answer pages. Fold them to the unit you are
checking. Write the number of correct answers in the score
box at the top of the unit page.

Hints for Better Understanding

◆ Units 1–12: Read the whole story. Then ask yourself, "Which
sentence is the sum of all the other sentences?" That will be
the main idea.

◆ Units 13–25: Read the story. Then figure out what the details
have in common. What is the writer trying to tell you?

Challenge Yourself

Try this challenge. Read each story. Answer the questions.
If the story has a main idea sentence, write a sentence using other
words to state the main idea. If the story does not contain a main
idea sentence, write one.

Writing

On pages 30 and 58, there are stories with questions. These
do not have answers for you to choose. Think of an answer.
Write it in your own words. On pages 31 and 59, you are asked
to write your own story. You are given a prewriting activity to
help you. You will find suggested answers on page 60. But your
answers may be very different.

1. Camp Fire is a group that helps young people. Both boys and girls can belong to it. Everyone in the group learns by doing things. Sometimes these young people camp outside and cook dinner over a fire. They also help people. At times they just have fun together. They learn how to share and make friends.

2. Too much of a good thing can sometimes be bad. This seems to be the case with California. The weather there is warm, dry, and never too hot or cold. It's easy to get to the ocean or to one of its many beaches. But now there are too many people living in California. Its roads are filled with cars. And its beaches are always too crowded.

3. Pet dogs do some things that wild dogs do. Wild dogs eat very quickly. They must eat quickly because the other animals can take their food away. Pet dogs don't usually have this problem, but they still eat quickly. Wild dogs have to make their own beds. So they walk around and around in the grass to make it flat. Pet dogs also turn around a few times before they lie down.

4. Most of us feel angry at times. Anger is a normal human feeling, like happiness or sadness. But anger can be harmful. There is a chance real anger might hurt others. Doctors say it can even make us sick. Counting to ten is a good way to cool our anger. Then we can think about things in a clear way.

5. Chalk comes from a one-celled animal that lives in the ocean. It has a shell made of lime. When the animal dies, its shell falls to the floor of the ocean. A layer of these shells builds up. It takes millions of years for one layer of shells to form. From this layer of shells comes a soft limestone used to make chalk.

_____ **1.** The story mainly tells
  A. when young people have fun
  B. who cooks over a camp fire
  C. how young people learn from Camp Fire
  D. how only girls belong to the group

_____ **2.** The story mainly tells
  A. which people moved to California
  B. how people love California too much
  C. when it's hard driving on the road
  D. how California beaches are dirty

_____ **3.** The story mainly tells
  A. who walks around in circles
  B. how pet dogs and wild dogs are alike
  C. how wild dogs make their beds
  D. how pet dogs eat slowly

_____ **4.** The story mainly tells
  A. why people get angry
  B. how to count to ten
  C. that anger can be harmful
  D. how to think clearly

_____ **5.** The story mainly tells
  A. how chalk is used
  B. where shells are made
  C. about the limestone used to make chalk
  D. about a one-celled animal

1. The first movies were made in black and white. There wasn't any color film at that time. Today some people are putting color on these old films. But others think that this practice should be stopped. They say that the old black-and-white movies should not be changed. They think the films are works of art and have a place in history.

2. Scientists can make plants glow in the dark. First they take a tiny part from a firefly. Then they put this part into a plant. Finally they use as water the same juice that fireflies use to glow. So at night the plant glows. Scientists hope to watch the light and learn more about how plants grow.

3. Some pilots are spies for the United States. The pilots fly around and watch for other planes. The pilots need to make sure that the other planes are from friendly countries. How do they do this? They use a small camera. This camera can take pictures of things that are many miles away.

4. The water in a pond or stream may look clean. But it could hold harmful matter that makes the water dirty. Not long ago, students on a field trip discovered pond frogs with strange bodies. Scientists are trying to find the cause. They think it might have something to do with the wastes in the water. But they have to prove it first.

5. Jean Du Sable was born in Haiti. He moved to Illinois and worked as a fur trader. Du Sable made many trips to Canada to bring back furs. He built a home on the spot he used as a lookout point. Settlers built stores near Du Sable. Then they built homes. Soon the area became a city. It was named Chicago. Du Sable was an African American. Now he is called the founder of Chicago.

_____ **1.** The story mainly tells
  A. what color the first movies were
  B. who is trying to color the old movies
  C. why old movies should not be changed
  D. which stars were in the first color movie

_____ **2.** The story mainly tells
  A. what makes fireflies glow at night
  B. who waters the plants
  C. how scientists make plants glow
  D. how scientists drink the plant juice

_____ **3.** The story mainly tells
  A. about the job of spy pilots
  B. how spy pilots destroy other planes
  C. how different kinds of cameras work
  D. what kinds of pictures cameras take

_____ **4.** The story mainly tells
  A. how dirty water might be harmful
  B. where to find frogs
  C. why ponds are bad
  D. who makes dirty water

_____ **5.** The story mainly tells
  A. about the man who founded the city of Chicago
  B. about fur trading
  C. how Chicago got its name
  D. where Jean Du Sable was born

1. An iguana is part of the lizard family. Marine iguanas are strange lizards. They are called diving dragons. They jump off rocks and dive into the water to find food. Now scientists have found an amazing fact about marine iguanas. Some can make themselves shrink when food is hard to find! When their food supply returns, they grow back to normal size.

2. People in China have a party on New Year's Day. At the party they eat only the foods they love. They say only happy things to each other. They visit with their best friends. All the Chinese people have a good time at the party. They hope that the rest of the year will be as good.

3. You have a cold. What should you eat? "Chicken soup," your grandmother would say. Now scientists are finding that Grandmother was right. Chicken soup is very good for you when you are sick. The chicken makes you stronger. The noodles help your body take in salt and water. You may need this extra salt and water when you are sick. Chicken soup just may be the perfect medicine.

4. Ellen Ochoa always loved to learn. As a child she read books and studied music. Learning can lead to great things. When she was older, Ellen's love for learning led her down a surprising path. She signed on as an astronaut! As she flew into the sky on the shuttle *Discovery*, Ellen Ochoa became the first Hispanic woman in space.

5. In 1902 Mary Bethune moved to Florida. She had only $1.50 in her purse. But she had a dream. She was a teacher. She wanted to start a school for young African Americans. Mary built her school. It was on what had once been a landfill. The school was Bethune College. It is now Bethune-Cookman College. Mary helped educate thousands of African Americans.

_____ **1.** The story mainly tells
  A. why marine iguanas are strange lizards
  B. what a diving dragon eats
  C. how iguanas shrink
  D. how an iguana finds food

_____ **2.** The story mainly tells
  A. which day is most important
  B. what the Chinese do on New Year's Day
  C. why some people have parties
  D. about the Chinese food at parties

_____ **3.** The story mainly tells
  A. whose grandmother was right
  B. how noodles in soup make you lose water
  C. how chicken soup is a kind of medicine
  D. how you shouldn't eat the chicken

_____ **4.** The story mainly tells
  A. how learning can lead to great things
  B. how Ellen read books
  C. how Ellen became an astronaut
  D. why Ellen Ochoa is older

_____ **5.** The story mainly tells
  A. what Bethune did with $1.50
  B. about Bethune's train ride
  C. which subjects are offered at the college
  D. how Bethune helped educate African Americans

1. Some people are born with dark spots on their faces. Other people get spots from being out in the sun too much. Most people who have spots don't like them. Doctors are now able to get rid of these spots. Doctors use a special gun that doesn't hurt the person. It just takes away the spots!

2. Buttons are useful. At first buttons were used only as ornaments. Once, a king of France had a coat with thousands of gold buttons sewn on it. Then someone had a new thought. Why not make a slit in cloth and push a button through it? Buttons began to hold pants up and keep shirts closed. Some buttons are tiny works of art. Collectors search for them.

3. Horse shows are the place to see beautiful horses. The riders and horses get scores for each event. First all the riders walk their horses around the ring. Then they trot the horses, making them go faster and faster. Finally they gallop. When they jump over logs or ponds, the riders must not fall. The best riders and horses get ribbons and prizes.

4. Many people are afraid of flying in airplanes. Sometimes they're so afraid that they get sick. This is a problem. These people can never visit friends who live far away. Doctors have started classes that teach people about planes. The people practice flying in planes. It works, too. Many people have learned to get over their fear of flying!

5. Fog and clouds are the same thing. But fog is a cloud on the ground. When a cloud is touching the earth or sea, it is called fog. Fog in the city is thicker than fog in the country. City air is full of dust. The dust mixes with the drops of water. It makes the fog thicker.

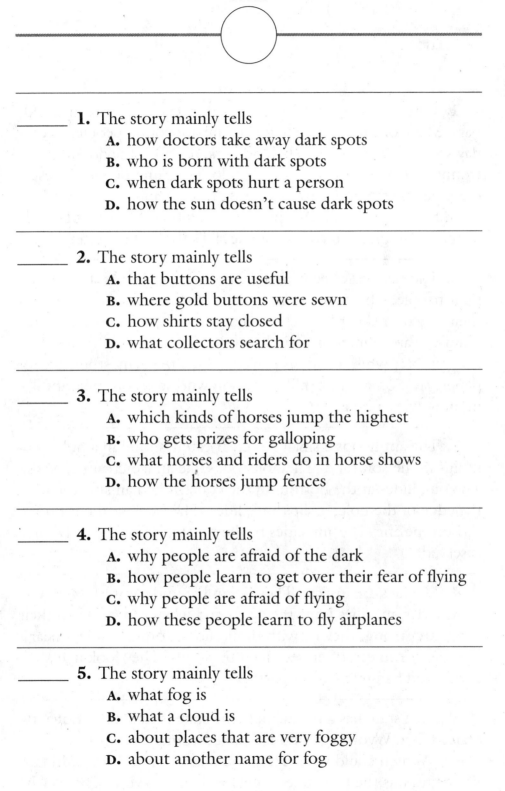

1. The story mainly tells
    A. how doctors take away dark spots
    B. who is born with dark spots
    C. when dark spots hurt a person
    D. how the sun doesn't cause dark spots

2. The story mainly tells
    A. that buttons are useful
    B. where gold buttons were sewn
    C. how shirts stay closed
    D. what collectors search for

3. The story mainly tells
    A. which kinds of horses jump the highest
    B. who gets prizes for galloping
    C. what horses and riders do in horse shows
    D. how the horses jump fences

4. The story mainly tells
    A. why people are afraid of the dark
    B. how people learn to get over their fear of flying
    C. why people are afraid of flying
    D. how these people learn to fly airplanes

5. The story mainly tells
    A. what fog is
    B. what a cloud is
    C. about places that are very foggy
    D. about another name for fog

UNIT 5

1. When people get into trouble, they can get locked behind bars. Many of those who are locked up are young people. Every day some older people go behind bars, too. But they're not in trouble. They go into the jails to help the young people. These older people teach the younger ones to read and write. They also teach them that people can be nice. Everyone hopes that this learning will give the young people skills to live life better.

2. The cakewalk began as a dance in 1900. It was started by poor people. The dancers pretended to be very fancy. It was their way of making fun of rich people. Today it is a circle game. Numbers are painted in a circle on the ground. People walk on the numbers while a song is played. When the song stops, the people stop on a number. The person who stops on the right number wins a cake!

3. The ant lion is a small insect. It catches food in a hole that it digs in the soft sand. The hole looks like an ice-cream cone. The bug hides at the bottom of the cone. When an ant reaches the edge of the hole, it slips and slides. The ant lion then throws dirt on the ant. The ant slides to the bottom of the hole. Dinner is served!

4. Mayflies are insects. They begin life underwater. As they grow older, mayflies leave the water and grow wings. When their wings are strong, they fly with thousands of other mayflies near the water. You can often see them by ponds. They look like a dark cloud hanging over the water.

5. Each state has a nickname. One state is called the Equality State. When Wyoming became a state, women and men were equal. Women could vote. They could also run for office. In fact Wyoming was the first state to give women the vote. That is why it's called the Equality State.

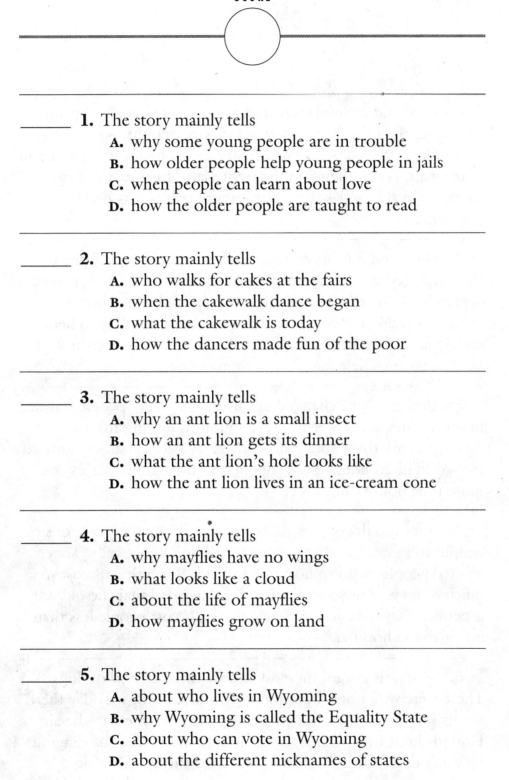

_____ **1.** The story mainly tells
  A. why some young people are in trouble
  B. how older people help young people in jails
  C. when people can learn about love
  D. how the older people are taught to read

_____ **2.** The story mainly tells
  A. who walks for cakes at the fairs
  B. when the cakewalk dance began
  C. what the cakewalk is today
  D. how the dancers made fun of the poor

_____ **3.** The story mainly tells
  A. why an ant lion is a small insect
  B. how an ant lion gets its dinner
  C. what the ant lion's hole looks like
  D. how the ant lion lives in an ice-cream cone

_____ **4.** The story mainly tells
  A. why mayflies have no wings
  B. what looks like a cloud
  C. about the life of mayflies
  D. how mayflies grow on land

_____ **5.** The story mainly tells
  A. about who lives in Wyoming
  B. why Wyoming is called the Equality State
  C. about who can vote in Wyoming
  D. about the different nicknames of states

1. Some butterflies lay their eggs on just one kind of plant. By tasting the plant, they know which one is right. Sometimes butterflies taste the wrong plant. So they fly to another plant and taste again. When they find the right plant, they lay their eggs there. Soon the eggs hatch. The hungry babies eat the plant their mother chose!

2. Kings and queens had the earliest zoos. They wanted to show off their money by keeping strange animals. Later, people kept animals in zoos because they wanted to learn about them. Students could take classes at the zoo. Today zoos try to help certain animals. These animals are disappearing from their wild homes. So zoos help keep these animals safe.

3. Airplanes have changed our lives. Long ago, people traveled in ships. They spent weeks or even months getting from one country to another. Today airplanes carry people halfway around the world in 15 hours. So we spend less time going places and more time doing things.

4. Years ago doctors made house calls. They took care of sick people at home. Later they stopped making house calls. They wanted people to go to hospitals instead. But hospitals cost so much money. Now some doctors have decided that the old way is better. They have found that house calls cost people less than going to the hospital.

5. A long time ago, there were only three groups of dogs. These were wise dogs, fighting dogs, and fast dogs. Today there are six groups of dogs. Sporting dogs hunt by smelling the air. Hounds hunt by smelling the ground. Terriers hunt by digging. Working dogs don't hunt. But they herd sheep and cattle. Toy dogs and nonsporting dogs make good friends for children and adults.

_____ **1.** The story mainly tells
    A. when baby butterflies come out of eggs
    B. how butterflies choose where to lay eggs
    C. what flies from one plant to another
    D. how butterflies always taste the right plant

_____ **2.** The story mainly tells
    A. how rulers showed off their money
    B. which people learned about zoo animals
    C. how zoos have changed over the years
    D. how animals will never disappear

_____ **3.** The story mainly tells
    A. how small the world was long ago
    B. how fast ships sailed around the world
    C. how airplanes changed our lives
    D. how people still travel on ships

_____ **4.** The story mainly tells
    A. which sick people go to hospitals
    B. why some doctors now go to people's houses
    C. when doctors changed their minds
    D. how much money doctors make today

_____ **5.** The story mainly tells
    A. how many dogs there are
    B. which is the best kind of dog
    C. about the ways dogs are grouped
    D. how dogs got their names

1. A man in Florida can talk to fish. He spent a long time learning how to do this. First he watched fish very closely. Then he listened to the noises they made. Finally he learned to make the same sounds. Sometimes the fish listen to him. At times he can even make them do things. This man thinks that someday fishermen might be able to call fish to their nets.

2. Sometimes people need help when they get older. Older people may need help in walking or in cooking their meals. At night they count on their families to do these things for them. But during the day, older people are left alone at home. To help them some cities have built day-care centers. Older people can go to these centers during the day. There they will get the help they need.

3. John Chapman planted apple trees in Ohio in the early 1800s. He carried the seeds all over the country. He sold the seeds or just gave them away to people. Chapman was a very kind man. He loved people, animals, and trees. The story of Johnny Appleseed is the story of his life.

4. Back in the 1700s, people often ate with their fingers. In England, the 4th Earl of Sandwich liked to keep his hands clean. One day he asked to have his food placed between two slices of bread. The sandwich was born. It was a great idea. Without it, lunches might be different today. We could be spreading our peanut butter and jelly on broccoli!

5. The state of Ohio got its name from a river. Native Americans called the big river *oheo*. *Oheo* means "beautiful." Settlers called it the Ohio River. Later the area north of the river became a state. The state was named after the beautiful river. It was called Ohio.

_____ **1.** The story mainly tells
    A. why fish listen to sounds
    B. who likes to fish
    C. how a man talks to fish
    D. how the fish never listen to this man

_____ **2.** The story mainly tells
    A. how older people can get the help they need
    B. who cooks meals for older people
    C. what families do at night
    D. who needs help walking

_____ **3.** The story mainly tells
    A. how apple trees grow from seeds
    B. where we get the story of Johnny Appleseed
    C. when Chapman lived in Ohio
    D. how Chapman traveled the country

_____ **4.** The story mainly tells
    A. how the sandwich was born
    B. how people used to eat
    C. why lunches might be different
    D. where to put peanut butter

_____ **5.** The story mainly tells
    A. how Ohio got its name
    B. where the Ohio River is
    C. how the Ohio River looks
    D. about a Native American word for *beautiful*

UNIT 8

1. The first dollhouses were built for grown-ups. These houses were as tall as people. They were also filled with pretty things. Rich people made these dollhouses look like their own homes. Only later did they build smaller dollhouses for children. Some of these are still around. They help us learn what real houses looked like long ago.

2. Mother ducks take baby ducks away from each other. This is the way it happens. The mother ducks take their babies swimming. Soon the pond is full of ducks. The mother ducks quack. They swim around the baby ducks. The mother duck that quacks loudest gets the greatest number of babies. Some mother ducks may have forty baby ducks. Others may have only two or three.

3. The African American man stared at the picture on the wall. It was a very old family picture. The man in the picture was a soldier. He died for his country. The eyes of the man in the picture seemed to ask, "Remember me?" But the young man thought, "No. People don't remember you." So he quit his job. He worked at passing a law that would put up a statue in Washington, D.C. The statue would honor the five thousand African Americans who died in the American Revolution.

4. Scientists have made a machine that has hands and eyes. This machine can see. It can also feel. How does it work? The machine sees through a camera. The camera moves, and it remembers what it sees. The machine feels by touching things with its metal arm. The wires in the arm can tell if things are hard or soft.

5. The distance between stars is too great to count in miles. So scientists use light-years. A light-year is the distance that light travels in one year. A light-year equals 5.9 trillion miles.

_____ **1.** The story mainly tells
    A. when people made dollhouses for children
    B. which dollhouses were the tallest
    C. what the first dollhouses were like
    D. which people didn't build dollhouses

_____ **2.** The story mainly tells
    A. which duck quacks the loudest
    B. how mother ducks take babies away
    C. when the ducks go swimming
    D. how baby ducks choose their mother

_____ **3.** The story mainly tells
    A. in which war the man in the picture died
    B. about a statue for African Americans
    C. who painted a picture
    D. that the statue honors only white men

_____ **4.** The story mainly tells
    A. why machines have hands and eyes
    B. who made a special machine
    C. how a machine sees and feels
    D. when scientists made this machine

_____ **5.** The story mainly tells
    A. how far it is between stars
    B. how fast light travels
    C. how big a star is
    D. about a light-year

1. Police use fingerprints to tell one person from another. Roses have fingerprints, too. But the prints aren't found on the pretty flowers. They're on the leaves. Each rose leaf has holes in it. The holes are like people's fingerprints. The holes of each different kind of rose have a special shape and size. By looking at the holes, people can tell the name of the rose.

2. Many families in Japan collect dolls. These families have a Doll Day for Girls and a Doll Day for Boys. On the girls' day, families bring out special dolls. The dolls are dressed as old kings and queens from Japan. On the boys' day, families bring out other dolls. The dolls are dressed as famous fighters from the past. These doll days are very special to the people of Japan.

3. It's hard to think of doctors as artists. But their job of healing people can be beautiful. For instance, doctors help people who can't hear well. In some cases doctors use a piece of a rib. They carve the rib so that it fits inside the ear. The bone is about a tenth of an inch high. It also has a pretty shape. With this bone in the ear, the person can hear much better.

4. Calamity Jane was a famous woman of the Wild West. She was famous because she was so tough. She lived during the 1800s. She learned to ride a horse and shoot a gun at an early age. People could always hear her coming. She also liked dressing in men's clothes. There weren't many women like Calamity Jane.

5. Cats are very much like lions and tigers. They can jump high in the air. Cats can jump seven feet straight up. They have padded feet. That way they can sneak up on their prey. Cats have 18 claws on their feet. They can push out and draw back their claws.

_____ **1.** The story mainly tells
　　　　A. what the holes in flowers are like
　　　　B. why flowers have fingerprints
　　　　C. how rose leaves have fingerprints
　　　　D. how all of the holes are the same size

_____ **2.** The story mainly tells
　　　　A. who plays with dolls in Japan
　　　　B. which dolls are famous in Japan
　　　　C. what doll days are like in Japan
　　　　D. how much the famous dolls cost

_____ **3.** The story mainly tells
　　　　A. how a doctor's work can be beautiful
　　　　B. who has tiny bones in their ears
　　　　C. why people lose their hearing
　　　　D. how to carve a rib

_____ **4.** The story mainly tells
　　　　A. why Calamity Jane was famous
　　　　B. how Calamity Jane dressed
　　　　C. when Calamity Jane rode a horse
　　　　D. when Calamity Jane was called a coward

_____ **5.** The story mainly tells
　　　　A. how a cat looks
　　　　B. about special things that a cat can do
　　　　C. how high a cat can jump
　　　　D. why a cat is a better pet than a dog

1. Every 11 years groups of dark spots show up on the sun. But the sunspots last for just a short time. Then they go away slowly. After 11 more years, the spots return. What exactly are these spots? Some scientists think that the spots are storms on the sun. They happen when the sun gets hotter. But they go away when the sun cools off again. Maybe the spots tell us when it's summer on the sun!

2. Many people like to fill their houses with plants. House plants look pretty. But caring for them can be hard. The plants often die indoors. Not getting enough water and sun is one thing that kills plants. So people have made new kinds of house plants. These new plants are real plants. But they have been dried. They aren't living, but they look alive. The dried plants look pretty, and people don't have to take care of them.

3. Linda Mastrandrea has been in a wheelchair for years. But she has never let problems stop her. Through hard work and exercise, she has become one of the top wheelchair athletes in the world. She has many gold medals for racing to prove it. Now she is a lawyer, too. Linda has worked hard in sports and in school.

4. Aardvarks are strange animals. They have short stumpy legs and huge donkey ears. Termites are their favorite feast. Aardvarks break open the termites' mounds with their strong claws. Humans would have to use a pickax to break these mounds. Soldier termites try to save the mound by biting the aardvarks. But it is useless. Aardvarks' stiff hair and tough skin help keep them safe.

5. Jupiter is the biggest planet in the galaxy. It is 88,600 miles around. Jupiter is thirteen hundred times the size of Earth. It weighs two and one-half times as much as the other eight planets put together!

_____ **1.** The story mainly tells
    A. why the sun gets hotter
    B. about sunspots
    C. where the worst storms are found
    D. how the spots show up only at night

_____ **2.** The story mainly tells
    A. who saves pretty plants
    B. how people have made new house plants
    C. why most house plants aren't alive
    D. how live plants are prettier than dried ones

_____ **3.** The story mainly tells
    A. how Linda never let problems stop her
    B. how Linda is a top athlete
    C. that Linda's medals are for racing
    D. that Linda is a lawyer

_____ **4.** The story mainly tells
    A. why aardvarks are strange animals
    B. what aardvarks eat
    C. why soldier termites bite
    D. about aardvarks' stiff hair

_____ **5.** The story mainly tells
    A. where Jupiter is located
    B. how big Jupiter is compared to Mars
    C. about the size of Jupiter
    D. how big Earth is

1. Children learn their first lessons in banking when they use piggy banks. Children put pennies in their banks and wait for the number of pennies to grow. The money is safe there. When the bank is full, the child can buy something with the money. In the same way, children's parents put their money in a real bank. It's safe there. They can add more money every month. Later they can use it to buy the things they need.

2. Have you ever wondered why hurricanes have names? The Weather Service said that names make reporting on storms easier. This helps them keep better records, too. At first only women's names were used. In 1979 men's names were added. There are six lists of names that are used. Sometimes a storm does so much harm that the storm's name is taken off the list.

3. Zoo elephants get very good care. Each morning zookeepers give them a special bath. They wash the elephants with water and a brush. Then they paint oil on their skin and rub oil on their feet. This is very important in elephant care. It helps the elephants stay healthy.

4. Not long ago, people raised their own chickens. They fed the chickens leftover food. They also gathered fresh eggs every day. Every morning the roosters awakened everybody. Sometimes the family cooked a chicken for dinner. Today life has changed. Most people buy chickens and eggs at stores. They have clocks to awaken them.

5. Migrant workers move from farm to farm. They work long hours for low pay. César Chávez was a migrant worker. He wanted to make the workers' lives better. He told people about the workers' problems and formed a union. Now their working conditions are better.

_____ **1.** The story mainly tells
  A. how children spend their money
  B. how a piggy bank is a lesson in banking
  C. when grown people put money in a bank
  D. why grown people don't use piggy banks

_____ **2.** The story mainly tells
  A. about reporting on storms
  B. why hurricanes have names
  C. when men's names were first used
  D. when names come off the list

_____ **3.** The story mainly tells
  A. why zookeepers have happy lives
  B. who paints oil on elephants
  C. why zookeepers give elephants special care
  D. how much elephants eat

_____ **4.** The story mainly tells
  A. that people once raised chickens
  B. why chickens give fresh eggs
  C. when the family cooked a chicken
  D. where the chicken pens were found

_____ **5.** The story mainly tells
  A. what crops migrant workers pick
  B. how much money a migrant worker makes
  C. that migrant workers work on farms
  D. about a man who helped migrant workers

1. Scientists use balloons to study the weather. They hook machines to balloons and send them up in the sky. The balloons rise in the sky until they finally pop. When this happens the machines fall to earth. Then scientists take these machines back to the lab to learn more about the weather.

2. People used to get together to build a barn. Families from all around would come to help. Barn building was like a big party. The women cooked a meal. The men worked together to pull up the sides of the barn and to build a roof. The women took care of the children and placed the meal on the tables. Everyone worked together. When the sun went down, a new barn stood shining and tall.

3. All winter long bears do nothing but sleep. To get ready for their winter sleep, they eat. They eat much food to get fat. The fat will become food their bodies will use while they sleep. Bears choose sleeping places such as caves. But they might also choose a hollow log or even a big pile of brush. If it gets warm on a winter day, the bears might come out to walk around. But they don't stay out long. Only in the spring do they finally get up and look for food.

4. Many farmers today grow fields of yellow sunflowers. People have many uses for sunflower seeds. After the seeds are dried and salted, people buy them to eat. Some sunflower seeds are pressed to make cooking oil. Some seeds are also ground to make a kind of butter.

5. James Fenimore Cooper wrote books in the 1800s. One day his wife was reading a book. He told her that he could write a better one. She dared him to do it. Cooper wrote his first book. He wrote many books about the people who settled America. He is the author of *The Deerslayer*.

_____ **1.** The story mainly tells
   A. about a machine that helps in the study of weather
   B. why scientists like to fly balloons
   C. how far the machines go up into the air
   D. how quickly the balloons pop

_____ **2.** The story mainly tells
   A. who cooked the food for the builders
   B. how helping by working together could be fun
   C. when all the men worked together
   D. how everyone hated the party

_____ **3.** The story mainly tells
   A. what kind of life a bear leads
   B. who likes caves for sleeping
   C. where bears sleep in the summer
   D. why bears love honey

_____ **4.** The story mainly tells
   A. why people eat salty seeds
   B. how sunflower seeds are of great value
   C. who uses cooking oil
   D. who likes sunflower butter

_____ **5.** The story mainly tells
   A. that Cooper's wife read many books
   B. that Cooper explored the American wilderness
   C. that Cooper was a writer in the 1800s
   D. that *The Deerslayer* was about James Cooper

Writing

Read each story. Think about the main idea. Write the main idea in your own words.

1. Helen Keller was blind and deaf. She could not speak as a child. But she learned how to speak. In fact, she learned how to speak English, French, and German. She was an amazing person!

What is the main idea of this story?

_____

_____

2. Skunks use a spray to protect themselves. This smelly spray can drive off animals and people. Skunks can squirt this liquid up to ten feet away. The odor is awful. But it helps. It keeps skunks free of danger.

What is the main idea of this story?

_____

_____

3. In 1926 Carter G. Woodson had an idea. He thought that African Americans should be honored. He called his idea "Negro History Week." The idea grew into Black History Month. And that's how Woodson became known as the Father of Black History.

What is the main idea of this story?

_____

_____

To check your answers, turn to page 60.

Prewriting

Think of a main idea that you would like to write about, such as an important person, an animal, or a hike in the woods. Fill in the chart below.

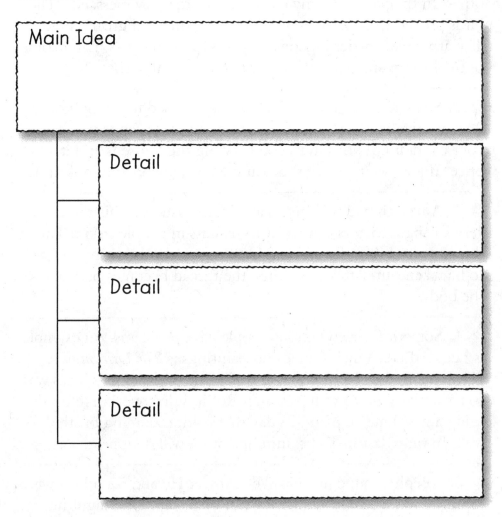

Main Idea

Detail

Detail

Detail

On Your Own

Now use another sheet of paper to write your story. Underline the sentence that tells the main idea.

To check your answers, turn to page 60.

1. There were times when soldiers had no way to talk to each other. In the past the army used pigeons to carry messages. The birds proved to be very brave. They flew through great danger. The army said carrier pigeons helped save many lives. Later some of the birds were given medals. They were real heroes.

2. Some signs can talk! These signs are used in selling houses. As you drive by the sign, a machine on the sign sends signals to your car radio. A voice tells you how big the house is and its price. If you want to buy the house, you can stop and look at it.

3. A new thread is being made from seashells. This thread is very strong. Doctors can use it to fix cuts in people's skin. The thread helps bring the cut skin back together. Also, it never has to be taken out. After some time the thread becomes part of the body.

4. Sometimes even famous people have problems. An example is Leonardo da Vinci. One of his paintings is *The Last Supper*. It was painted in 1495 on a big wall. One of da Vinci's ideas was to try a new kind of wall painting. But it didn't work. He tried using a new kind of paint. Today that paint is coming off the wall. In time da Vinci's beautiful painting will disappear.

5. Joseph Cinque lived in West Africa. He and 52 others were captured to be slaves. They were put on a ship. One night he escaped from his chains. He and his friends took over the ship. They did not want to become slaves. They wanted to sail back to their home. But the ship was forced to land in the United States. Cinque took his case to the Supreme Court. The Court ruled that Cinque could go back home to Africa.

_____ **1.** The story mainly tells
    A. how pigeons carry messages
    B. why pigeons were brave
    C. how pigeons helped the army
    D. how birds were given medals

_____ **2.** The story mainly tells
    A. where to find big houses
    B. how some signs can help sell houses
    C. about the price of the house
    D. how signals are sent to your house

_____ **3.** The story mainly tells
    A. why thread made of seashells is used to fix cuts
    B. how thread is made into cloth
    C. how cuts in the skin get well
    D. how doctors take out the thread

_____ **4.** The story mainly tells
    A. how da Vinci's new idea wasn't a good one
    B. why da Vinci painted
    C. how great da Vinci was
    D. how da Vinci became famous after he died

_____ **5.** The story mainly tells
    A. about a man who fought against slavery
    B. about a ship ride
    C. about life as a slave
    D. about life in West Africa

1. Throw away those skin creams! Doctors say that skin creams don't really help your skin look younger. They say there's a better way to keep your skin looking young. It doesn't cost a penny. Just stay out of the sun during the hottest part of the day. If you must be in the sun, stay out for only a short time. Also, be sure to wear sunscreen and a hat to shade your face.

2. We all know that babies make funny sounds. Little by little, babies learn that some sounds will call their mother and father. Other sounds will get them food. Yet some sounds will bring them nothing at all. Babies learn to talk by finding out which sounds work best.

3. Many robbers look for an easy way to make money. They don't want to spend much time breaking into your house. So to keep robbers away, you should put locks on all your doors. Put sticks in the runners of all sliding windows. Close the curtains at night so that no one can see inside the house. Also, always lock your house when you leave.

4. Baseball players have to step up to get onto the field. They must step down when their side is out. Their dugouts are built half below the ground. They are made like that for good reasons. If dugouts were tall, the fans who sit behind them could not see the game. Lower dugouts would be a problem for the players. They would need a stepladder to see the game.

5. Today Emily Dickinson is a famous poet. But she was not known as a poet during her life. Dickinson wrote a few poems. She sent them to a magazine contest. They were turned down. After that, she never tried to publish her poems. When she died, her poems were found. Now people read hundreds of her poems.

_____ **1.** The story mainly tells
  A. about easy ways to take care of your skin
  B. why skin creams are good for you
  C. how long you should stay out in the sun
  D. how wearing a hat doesn't help

_____ **2.** The story mainly tells
  A. which babies make the loudest noises
  B. how babies learn to talk
  C. when babies first start to make noise
  D. how babies aren't smart

_____ **3.** The story mainly tells
  A. who robbers are
  B. how to make your house safe from robbers
  C. how to close the curtains
  D. how locks aren't a good idea

_____ **4.** The story mainly tells
  A. where baseball players sit
  B. when baseball players must step down
  C. why dugouts are built the way they are
  D. who needs a stepladder

_____ **5.** The story mainly tells
  A. about a woman's fame as a poet after her death
  B. how to write hundreds of poems
  C. how to get your poems published
  D. how Emily Dickinson got her poems published

1. Long ago Jane Addams didn't believe that poor people were treated fairly. She wanted a law that would keep poor children from having to work. She also thought that poor women shouldn't have to work more than eight hours a day. Many of her wishes became laws.

2. Everyone knows the kind of ham people eat. But another ham is the person who runs a radio station for fun. Hams use radios to talk to other hams, even in other countries. What happens if two hams don't speak the same language? Hams have made a new language that all hams learn. It's called the Q signal language because everything starts with a Q. For instance, "QTH?" means "Where are you?"

3. Everything is made up of tiny things called atoms. How small are atoms? Take out a pencil. Make a tiny dot on this page. Now sharpen your pencil. Make an even smaller dot on the page. The tiniest dot that you could make would be made of millions of atoms. That's how small atoms are!

4. There's a man who grew up wanting to become a postmaster. As a boy he always dreamed of working for a post office. When he finished school, his wish came true. He became the postmaster of a little town in Iowa. It seemed like the perfect job except for one little thing. About half the people in his town have the same last name. The other half have another last name!

5. Langston Hughes loved to write. He is best known as a poet. But he also wrote plays, songs, and books. Hughes wrote in a warm and funny way. He wrote about ordinary African Americans. He is known around the world as one of America's best writers.

_____ **1.** The story mainly tells
   A. how Jane Addams worked to help the poor
   B. why people are poor
   C. when children should work long hours
   D. how poor people were treated fairly

_____ **2.** The story mainly tells
   A. about a new language for hams everywhere
   B. who listens to radios
   C. about different kinds of meat
   D. how radio hams like to eat ham

_____ **3.** The story mainly tells
   A. that atoms are so small we can't even see them
   B. where to put a dot
   C. what a pencil is made of
   D. how an atom is bigger than a dot

_____ **4.** The story mainly tells
   A. what the name of the town is
   B. what working for a post office is like
   C. how one postmaster has a problem
   D. how people have too many names

_____ **5.** The story mainly tells
   A. why Langston Hughes loved to write
   B. about Langston Hughes's most famous poem
   C. when Langston Hughes lived
   D. about a famous American writer

1. Katherine Anne Porter was born in Texas in 1890. She did not go to college, but she read many books. Porter wrote stories. But people wanted her to write a book. Her first book took twenty years to write. It was *Ship of Fools*. It was a big seller. Later it was made into a movie.

2. Neil Armstrong was an astronaut. In 1969 he did something no one else had done before. He set foot on the moon. He said, "That's one small step for a man, one giant leap for mankind." Edwin Aldrin followed Armstrong. They placed an American flag on the moon.

3. Air is filled with invisible water vapor. The vapor freezes when it meets the cold ground. It forms a thin layer of ice crystals. It covers the ground with a thin, white layer. This is called frost.

4. Earthquakes happen in places where there are great cracks in the rocks below the ground. The rocks on each side of the crack slide past each other. Suddenly the ground begins to shake. The shaking lasts for a few seconds or even minutes. Buildings sometimes fall down. The rocks settle. Then the earthquake is over.

5. Centipedes are not insects. But they look like insects. They are long animals with short legs. *Centipede* means "hundred feet." But centipedes have 350 legs! Millipedes also have many legs. *Millipede* means "thousand feet." But they have about 700 legs!

_____ **1.** The story mainly tells
   A. about Porter's first book
   B. that Porter was a Texan
   C. that Porter liked to go to the movies
   D. that Porter wrote many books

_____ **2.** The story mainly tells
   A. what Neil Armstrong said on the moon
   B. who first walked on the moon
   C. how Armstrong and Aldrin reached the moon
   D. what clothing Armstrong wore on the moon

_____ **3.** The story mainly tells
   A. where water vapor comes from
   B. how ice forms
   C. where snow comes from
   D. how frost is formed

_____ **4.** The story mainly tells
   A. what happens during an earthquake
   B. about the San Francisco earthquake
   C. what to do during an earthquake
   D. how to stop an earthquake

_____ **5.** The story mainly tells
   A. how many legs centipedes and millipedes have
   B. what kind of animal a centipede is
   C. that centipedes have one hundred legs
   D. that millipedes have one thousand legs

1. Settlers nearly died trying to cross Death Valley. The valley lies in two states. It is located in California and Nevada. Death Valley is a desert. It's the hottest place in North America. It's also the lowest point. It lies 282 feet below sea level. Settlers gave the valley its name.

2. Greenland is a cold country. Most of it is covered with ice and snow. It is a white land. When explorers first found Greenland, they saw green grass. They named the place Greenland. Then they discovered that only the coast is green.

3. The bee hummingbird is the size of a bee. This bird is two and one-half inches long. It weighs the same as a lump of sugar. It has a long beak. This tiny bird lives in Cuba.

4. Lucy Stone wanted to go to college. Her father thought women shouldn't go to school. So Lucy saved her money. She was the first Massachusetts woman to earn a college degree. She worked to give women the right to vote. She ran a newspaper. Many ideas of the women's movement were found in this newspaper. When Lucy married she kept her maiden name. She was the first woman in America to do this. Lucy died in 1893. Women got the right to vote 27 years later.

5. The word *nevada* is Spanish for "snow covered." The Sierra Nevada is a mountain range in the western United States. Nevada is a state in that part of the country. It was named after these snow-covered mountains.

_____ **1.** The story mainly tells
     A. what life is like in Death Valley
     B. how Death Valley got its name
     C. how Death Valley lies 282 feet above sea level
     D. how Death Valley stretches into three states

_____ **2.** The story mainly tells
     A. what the weather is like in Greenland
     B. where Greenland is located
     C. how Greenland got its name
     D. that Greenland is an island

_____ **3.** The story mainly tells
     A. about a kind of bee
     B. how a hummingbird is like a bee
     C. about the smallest insect
     D. about the bee hummingbird

_____ **4.** The story mainly tells
     A. that Lucy Stone started a newspaper
     B. that Lucy Stone went to college
     C. that Lucy Stone lived in Massachusetts
     D. that Lucy Stone worked hard for women's rights

_____ **5.** The story mainly tells
     A. the meaning of Spanish words
     B. how Nevada got its name
     C. that it snows often in Nevada
     D. about the mountains of Nevada

1. One kind of spider makes a web underwater. It weaves its web in water plants. Then it carries bubbles of air down to fill the web. The water spider lies still on its web. Soon a water insect swims near it. The spider dashes out and catches the insect. It brings its catch back to the air-filled web to eat.

2. Two things make a tree a conifer. It must make seeds in its cones. It must also have needlelike leaves. Conifers are called evergreen trees. They look green all the time. Conifers lose and replace their leaves. But they never lose all their leaves at the same time.

3. This book is read by sight. Braille is read by touch. Braille letters are made up of raised dots. People who are blind read by running their fingers over the letters. Braille was named after the man who invented it. Louis Braille invented Braille in 1829.

4. Hair has color because it contains melanin. Dark hair has much melanin in it. Light hair has less. As people grow older, their hair has less melanin. But the hair keeps growing. So the hair looks gray or white because it doesn't have any melanin.

5. One day Frank Baum was telling a story to some children. He told about a girl named Dorothy. She was swept from her home to a strange land. It was a magical place. One of the children asked Baum about the name of the strange land. He looked around the room. He saw a filing cabinet. One drawer was labeled A–G. The next was labeled H–N. The last drawer was O–Z. He looked at the last drawer and named the land Oz. Baum later wrote the book *The Wonderful Wizard of Oz.*

_____ **1.** The story mainly tells
  A. what a water spider looks like
  B. how a water spider builds its web
  C. what the spider does with water insects
  D. how one kind of spider lives under the water

_____ **2.** This story mainly tells
  A. another name for the evergreen tree
  B. about conifer trees
  C. about different types of conifer trees
  D. when conifer trees lose their leaves

_____ **3.** This story mainly tells
  A. how Louis Braille invented Braille
  B. how to read Braille
  C. about a special kind of writing for people who are blind
  D. how to read this book

_____ **4.** This story mainly tells
  A. how hair grows
  B. how to change the color of hair
  C. where melanin comes from
  D. why hair is light or dark

_____ **5.** This story mainly tells
  A. how Baum named the land of Oz
  B. where Dorothy lived
  C. how Baum named Dorothy
  D. when Baum wrote *The Wonderful Wizard of Oz*

1. Frederick Douglass was born a slave. He escaped to freedom. Douglass spoke out against slavery. He wanted it to end. He explained that many slaves were whipped or killed. He told about children being taken from their parents and sold. Douglass became a famous speaker. He also started a newspaper. In it he wrote about ending slavery.

2. If you spill ink on a shirt, it won't come out. If you spill ink on your skin, you can wash it off. The ink comes off in a layer of cells. Skin is made up of thirty layers of cells. Washing your skin removes a layer of cells. When one layer of skin is removed, it is replaced by the layer below it. New cells grow so that there are always thirty layers.

3. Cork is the outer bark of the cork oak tree. Most cork oak trees grow in Spain and Portugal. When the tree is twenty years old, the bark is stripped off. Then it is seasoned and boiled. The bark is boiled to soften it and take out the acids. Next it is dried in flat sheets. The cork sheets are shipped all over the world. They are made into bottle stoppers, bulletin boards, and other things.

4. A fly has six feet. Each foot has a plump little pad on the bottom. The pads flatten out when the fly walks on a smooth surface. They give off a sticky liquid that holds the fly to the wall or the ceiling. The liquid acts like glue so that the fly doesn't fall.

5. Polo is one of the oldest of all sports. It was started in Persia in 500 B.C. The players ride horses. They hit a ball with a wooden mallet. Each period of play is called a chukka. It lasts seven minutes. There are eight chukkas in one game.

_____ **1.** The story mainly tells
    A. when Douglass lived
    B. that Douglass worked hard to end slavery
    C. that Douglass was a slave
    D. that Douglass fought in the Civil War

_____ **2.** The story mainly tells
    A. how skin can be washed
    B. how to get ink out of a tablecloth
    C. about cells that make up layers of skin
    D. how often to wash skin

_____ **3.** The story mainly tells
    A. how cork is used in Spain and Portugal
    B. that cork oak trees can be twenty years old
    C. how long it takes to make cork
    D. how cork oak bark is made into useful things

_____ **4.** The story mainly tells
    A. how many legs a fly has
    B. about the fly's special feet
    C. how flies make glue
    D. about different types of flies

_____ **5.** The story mainly tells
    A. about a very old sport
    B. what kind of horses are used in polo
    C. what a polo mallet is made of
    D. how long a chukka lasts

1. A set is the place in which a movie is filmed. Carpenters build sets to show scenes where the action takes place. Some sets are painted to look like real rooms. They can be used for plays, films, or television shows. Sets can also be built to look like the outdoors. A set for a whole street or town can even be built.

2. A family tree doesn't grow in the yard. This kind of chart shows the members of a family. Some people wonder about their roots. They like tracing their ancestors. When they chart a family tree, they can see how branches of their family formed. Sometimes exciting stories about ancestors come to light. A family tree is a lot of work, but it is great fun, too.

3. When Ethel Waters was a child, she was poor. She worked as a maid for five dollars a day. Ethel knew she was talented. She began singing. She worked very hard. She sang and acted in movies and plays. In 1950 Ethel Waters won an award for acting in a play. She became known as the actress with the golden voice.

4. A chameleon is a kind of lizard. Its skin is clear, but it can change color. Under its skin are layers of cells. These cells have yellow, black, and red color in them. Anger makes these colors darken. Fear makes them lighten. It also makes yellow spots appear. Temperature and light can also cause these colors to change. These changes make the chameleon hard to see. Changing colors can save a chameleon's life.

5. Rice is grown in a different way from many other crops. Young rice plants are planted in flooded fields. These fields of water are called paddies. The rice plants grow in two to four inches of water. Rice has long leaves and clusters of flowers. The flowers turn into grains of rice and are collected.

_____ **1.** The story mainly tells
     A. how television shows and movies are made
     B. that films are made outdoors
     C. how sets are used
     D. that carpenters build sets

_____ **2.** The story mainly tells
     A. what a family tree is
     B. how people wonder about their roots
     C. how family branches are formed
     D. how stories about ancestors come to light

_____ **3.** The story mainly tells
     A. that Ethel Waters was poor
     B. where Ethel Waters grew up
     C. about a famous maid
     D. how Ethel Waters became famous

_____ **4.** The story mainly tells
     A. that a chameleon has clear skin
     B. how a chameleon's skin can change color
     C. where chameleons live
     D. that sometimes a chameleon has yellow spots

_____ **5.** The story mainly tells
     A. about ways to cook rice
     B. how rice plants grow
     C. how rice is collected
     D. why the rice fields are flooded

1. Sometimes deep in the ocean, an earthquake shakes the ocean floor. The movement starts a tidal wave. At first the wave is small. But it can move toward the shore at a speed of up to five hundred miles per hour. It makes a huge wave as it reaches the coast. The tidal wave hits the land with great force. It can destroy everything in its path.

2. Pluto is the ninth planet in our solar system. It is the farthest planet from the sun. Pluto is smaller than any other planet that moves around the sun. It is about eighteen hundred miles around. It is smaller than Earth's moon.

3. Clara Barton worked as a nurse in the Civil War. She traveled with the Union Army. After the war she headed a search for missing soldiers. When the search ended, she went to Europe. There she worked with the European Red Cross. After she came home, she wanted to start a Red Cross in America. She worked very hard. Later she became its president. She worked with the Red Cross for 23 years.

4. Water has great power. Waves beat at rock shores day after day. The waves carve out caves in the rock. Underground streams flow through rock. The water slowly wears away the rock. The streams carve out underground caves.

5. Camels have one or two humps on their backs. The humps are made of fat. The fat stores energy. When there isn't much food, the camel lives off the energy from its humps.

_____ **1.** The story mainly tells
      A. that earthquakes happen on the ocean floor
      B. how fast a tidal wave moves
      C. another name for a tidal wave
      D. how a tidal wave is formed

_____ **2.** The story mainly tells
      A. how Pluto got its name
      B. how big Pluto is compared to Earth
      C. about the size of Pluto
      D. how far away Pluto is from the sun

_____ **3.** The story mainly tells
      A. where Clara Barton lived
      B. why Clara Barton became a nurse
      C. about Clara Barton's work with the Red Cross
      D. that Clara Barton worked in Europe

_____ **4.** The story mainly tells
      A. where caves are found
      B. how water forms caves
      C. how tides affect caves
      D. how water breaks rock

_____ **5.** The story mainly tells
      A. about the humps of camels
      B. how many humps a camel has
      C. how much fat is in a camel's humps
      D. how heavy a camel's humps can be

1. A flying fish swims along the surface of the water. It beats its tail to build up speed. Then it spreads its fins like wings. It flies into the air at about forty miles per hour. The flying fish flies over the waves. It flies to escape from bigger fish.

2. Jim Thorpe played baseball during the summer before the Olympics. His team gave him food and a place to live while he was playing for them. Thorpe entered events in the Olympics and won two gold medals. But the judges said that athletes could not play sports for money and also be in the Olympic Games. So they took Thorpe's gold medals away from him. Thorpe did not think it was fair. He did not make any money while he was playing baseball. He was only given food and a place to live. Thorpe fought to get his medals back. After he died the Olympic officials decided that he had been right. They gave his medals to his children.

3. A person who sews clothes is a tailor. One kind of bird is good at sewing. This bird is called the tailor bird. It sews a nest for itself. The tailor bird uses its beak to punch holes in the edges of leaves. Then it threads a piece of spider web through the holes. It pulls the leaves together and knots the thread. This makes a cup-shaped nest. The tailor bird lines the nest with cotton or grass.

4. The liquid found in your mouth is called saliva. Saliva helps you swallow food. It makes your throat slippery. Saliva helps you taste food. The saliva dissolves food so that the tongue can taste it. Saliva also helps your body digest food.

5. A meteor is a small, stony chunk that speeds through space. When it enters Earth's atmosphere, it gets very hot. It is so hot that it glows. It looks like a star falling through the sky. Some meteors burn up as they fall and land in the oceans.

_____ **1.** The story mainly tells
- **A.** where flying fish live
- **B.** how a big fish catches a flying fish
- **C.** how flying fish can fly
- **D.** how flying fish eat

_____ **2.** The story mainly tells
- **A.** why the judges took away Thorpe's Olympic medals
- **B.** about the Olympics
- **C.** which year Thorpe was in the Olympics
- **D.** that Thorpe was a good baseball player

_____ **3.** The story mainly tells
- **A.** why this bird is called a tailor bird
- **B.** how the tailor bird lines its nest
- **C.** what a tailor bird's nest is called
- **D.** where the tailor bird is found

_____ **4.** The story mainly tells
- **A.** another name for saliva
- **B.** where saliva comes from
- **C.** how saliva is useful
- **D.** how the tongue tastes food

_____ **5.** The story mainly tells
- **A.** how a meteor is made
- **B.** about the size of a meteor
- **C.** the difference between a meteor and a star
- **D.** about a meteor entering Earth's atmosphere

1. Alex Haley wanted to know about his family's roots. Haley traced his roots to Africa. He wrote a book based on his family history. In the book he talked about life in Africa and life as a slave in America. He told how one family found freedom. The title of Haley's book is *Roots*. Later it was made into a movie. *Roots* made people want to know about their own family history.

2. Warm air mixed with moisture rises into the sky. It rises into air that is cool. The cool air can't hold all the moisture. So the moisture that the air cannot hold turns into tiny drops of water. If the air is very cold, the moisture changes to bits of ice. The water and ice form clouds.

3. Mars is called the Red Planet. It is the fourth planet from the Sun. From Earth it looks like a bright, red star. Its surface is made of red soil and rock. Red dust floats in its atmosphere. The dust makes the whole planet look red.

4. Deserts are found all over Earth. They are very dry. Winds mostly blow away from a desert. The winds blow away any damp air. This is why it hardly ever rains in the desert.

5. Pumice is a rock that can float on water. Pumice is not solid. It has bubbles of air inside. Pumice is formed from lava. Lava is the liquid rock that pours from a volcano. The lava bubbles and then cools to form pumice.

_____ **1.** The story mainly tells
   A. about Haley's family
   B. that *Roots* was a famous movie
   C. about the number of books Haley wrote
   D. about a famous book written by Haley

_____ **2.** The story mainly tells
   A. why warm air rises
   B. at what height warm air cools
   C. how clouds are formed
   D. why some clouds are rain clouds

_____ **3.** The story mainly tells
   A. about a red star
   B. why Mars is called the Red Planet
   C. why rocks on Mars are red
   D. that you can see Mars from Earth

_____ **4.** The story mainly tells
   A. why it is dry in deserts
   B. that winds bring rain
   C. about deserts that are found in the United States
   D. when it last rained in a desert

_____ **5.** The story mainly tells
   A. what lava is
   B. how pumice is used
   C. why pumice can float
   D. how pumice looks

1. Henry González wanted to run for the Texas legislature. He went to political leaders for help. They said that a Mexican American could not win. But he ran anyway. He spent $300 on his campaign. The other men who ran spent much more money. González lost the election. But he lost by only a few votes. Then González ran for city council and won. He went on to win other state and national offices.

2. Pigskin is very sensitive. It sunburns very easily. This is why pigs don't lie in the sun. They lie in the shade. They roll around in the mud to cover their skin from the sun.

3. Dixy Lee Ray wanted to become governor. People laughed at her. There had been only four women governors in the United States. All had been elected with the help of their husbands. But Ray had never been married. She ran for governor on her own. Ray became the first woman governor of Washington.

4. When an io moth is resting, its wings are folded. If the moth sees a hungry bird, it unfolds its wings. The wings have markings called eyespots. Each spot looks like a big eye. The eyespots scare the bird away.

5. Athletes who are disabled wanted a place to show their skills in sports. The Olympics gave them a good idea. Now they have the Paralympics. These events in sports are held during the same year as the Olympics. The host country that year holds the Paralympics, too. Athletes from around the world can set out to "go for the gold." Now many more young men and women are going for the gold.

_____ **1.** The story mainly tells
   A. about a man who became a political leader
   B. that González lived in Texas
   C. about González's high-priced campaign
   D. how political leaders helped González

_____ **2.** The story mainly tells
   A. how pigs keep from getting sunburned
   B. what pigs do in the sun
   C. where pigs live
   D. how pigskin is made

_____ **3.** The story mainly tells
   A. about the first woman governor in the
      United States
   B. why Dixy Lee Ray wanted to become governor
   C. about a woman who ran her own campaign
   D. who Dixy Lee Ray's husband was

_____ **4.** The story mainly tells
   A. which animals have eyespots
   B. about the size of eyespots
   C. how an io moth protects itself
   D. about the color of an io moth

_____ **5.** The story mainly tells
   A. about sports skills of people who are disabled
   B. what the Paralympics are
   C. who the host country is
   D. about the Olympics

1. Marina López was sick. Her doctors said that walking would be good for her health. She and her husband began playing golf. Their daughter, Nancy, would go with them to the golf course. They would let her hit the ball. They noticed that she could hit the ball long distances. Nancy won a golf tournament when she was nine years old. By the time she was 12, she had won a state women's tournament. Nancy became a professional golfer when she was 19. Nancy López is now in the golfer's hall of fame.

2. King Louis XIV of France was a short man. He wanted to look taller. So he ordered high heels for his shoes. Then he had his shoes trimmed with lace, bows, and jewels. One pair of shoes had bows that were 16 inches wide. He had artists paint scenes on the heels of his shoes. Soon other men in France wore high-heeled shoes with flowers and bows.

3. People pick the ripe fruit of the soapberry tree. They cut up the fruit. Then they mix it with cold water from a stream or lake. The fruit fills the water with suds. These suds are used to wash clothes.

4. The Loch Ness Monster has been seen many times. It lives in a lake in Scotland called Loch Ness. The waters of Loch Ness are the color of coffee. So no one has been able to take a clear picture of the monster or catch it. The monster is said to be about twenty feet long. It has a tiny head and a long neck. Its big body has flippers and many humps.

5. Trees are cut down and chopped into tiny chips. The wood chips are cooked in water and chemicals. They make a pulp that looks like oatmeal. The pulp is squeezed until it is very thin and flat. It is dried to make a giant sheet of paper. Paper can also be made from cotton fibers.

_____ **1.** The story mainly tells
    A. how many tournaments Nancy López has won
    B. how Marina López's health improved
    C. how Nancy López started playing golf
    D. that Nancy López's mother was a famous golfer

_____ **2.** The story mainly tells
    A. about King Louis XIV's high heels
    B. how tall King Louis XIV was
    C. how the king painted his heels
    D. about shoes that men wear today

_____ **3.** The story mainly tells
    A. where soapberry trees are found
    B. about a natural laundry soap
    C. about the many uses of the soapberry tree
    D. about washing clothes

_____ **4.** The story mainly tells
    A. that the monster does not exist
    B. how many people have seen the monster
    C. where Loch Ness is located
    D. how no one has proved that the monster is real

_____ **5.** The story mainly tells
    A. how paper is made
    B. what wood pulp is
    C. how many trees it takes to make a sheet of paper
    D. how cotton fibers are turned into paper

Writing

Read each story. Think about the main idea. Write the main idea in your own words.

1. Mary Myers liked to go up in balloons. She wanted to be her own pilot. In 1880 she did just that. Her balloon took off from Little Falls, New York. Mary became the first woman balloon pilot. After that many women flew alone in their own balloons.

What is the main idea of this story?

_____

_____

2. Beto lived in the city. But one summer he visited his Uncle Alex on the farm. That summer Beto learned how to ride horses. Now Beto is grown up. He rides horses in races. He is a famous jockey. And he says he owes it all to his Uncle Alex.

What is the main idea of this story?

_____

_____

3. People have learned much about the oceans. They learned through exploring oceans. But oceans are huge. And they are very deep. So there is much more to learn. There still are many questions about life in the oceans.

What is the main idea of the this story?

_____

_____

To check your answers, turn to page 60.

Prewriting

Think of a main idea that you would like to write about, such as visiting a farm, flying in a balloon, or exploring the ocean. Fill in the chart below.

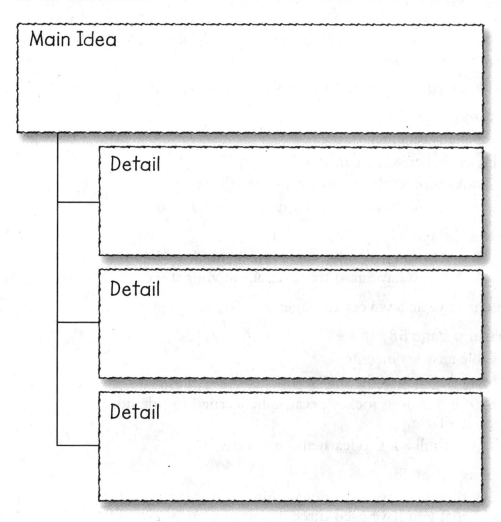

Main Idea

Detail

Detail

Detail

On Your Own

Now use another sheet of paper to write your story. Underline the sentence that tells the main idea.

To check your answers, turn to page 60.

Check Yourself

Using What You Know, Page 3
Answers will vary.

Practice Finding the Main Idea, Page 4
The correct answer is B. There are details about the Sahara's location, rainfall, and temperature. If you add these details together, you will get the main idea.

To check your answers to pages 6–29, see page 61.

Writing, Page 30
Possible answers include:
1. Helen Keller was an amazing person.
2. Skunks protect themselves with a smelly spray.
3. Carter G. Woodson is the Father of Black History.

Writing, Page 31
Check that you have underlined your main idea.
Check that you have used three details in your story.

To check your answers to pages 32–57, see page 62.

Writing, Page 58
Possible answers include:
1. Mary Myers was the first woman balloon pilot.
2. Beto is a famous jockey because he learned to ride horses at his uncle's farm.
3. There's still a lot to learn about oceans.

Writing, Page 59
Check that you have underlined your main idea.
Check that you have used three details in your story.

Steck-Vaughn • Comprehension Skills Series

Check Yourself

Unit 1 pp. 6–7	Unit 2 pp. 8–9	Unit 3 pp. 10–11	Unit 4 pp. 12–13	Unit 5 pp. 14–15	Unit 6 pp. 16–17	Unit 7 pp. 18–19	Unit 8 pp. 20–21	Unit 9 pp. 22–23	Unit 10 pp. 24–25	Unit 11 pp. 26–27	Unit 12 pp. 28–29
1. C	1. C	1. A	1. A	1. B	1. B	1. C	1. C	1. C	1. B	1. B	1. A
2. B	2. C	2. B	2. A	2. C	2. C	2. A	2. B	2. C	2. B	2. B	2. B
3. B	3. A	3. C	3. C	3. B	3. C	3. B	3. B	3. A	3. A	3. C	3. A
4. C	4. A	4. A	4. B	4. C	4. B	4. A	4. C	4. A	4. A	4. A	4. B
5. C	5. A	5. D	5. A	5. B	5. C	5. A	5. D	5. B	5. C	5. D	5. C

Unit 13 pp. 32–33	Unit 14 pp. 34–35	Unit 15 pp. 36–37	Unit 16 pp. 38–39	Unit 17 pp. 40–41	Unit 18 pp. 42–43	Unit 19 pp. 44–45	Unit 20 pp. 46–47	Unit 21 pp. 48–49	Unit 22 pp. 50–51	Unit 23 pp. 52–53	Unit 24 pp. 54–55	Unit 25 pp. 56–57
1. C	1. A	1. A	1. A	1. B	1. D	1. B	1. C	1. D	1. C	1. D	1. A	1. C
2. B	2. B	2. A	2. B	2. C	2. B	2. C	2. A	2. C	2. A	2. C	2. A	2. A
3. A	3. B	3. A	3. D	3. D	3. C	3. D	3. D	3. C	3. A	3. B	3. C	3. B
4. A	4. C	4. C	4. A	4. D	4. D	4. B	4. B	4. B	4. C	4. A	4. C	4. D
5. A	5. A	5. D	5. A	5. B	5. A	5. A	5. B	5. A	5. D	5. C	5. B	5. A